DATE DUE

# Ballpark

## ELISHA COOPER

Greenwillow Books    New York

It's morning at the ballpark on the day of the game.
A lone groundskeeper on a red tractor mows the outfield.

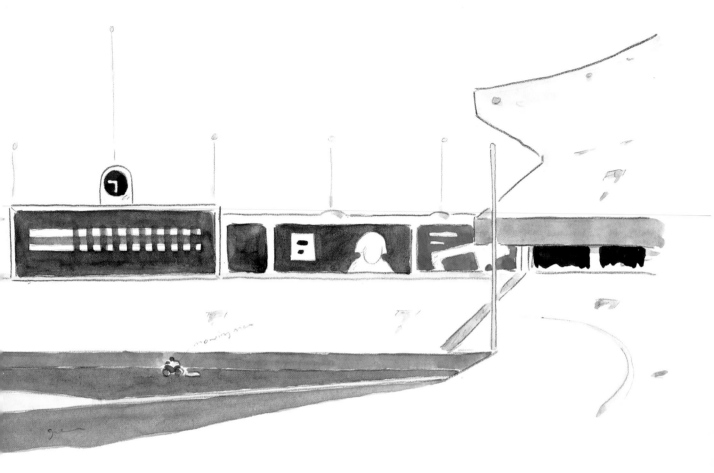

When he stops, he kneels and smoothes the grass
with his palm, plucks a few strands, and tastes them.

At the entrance to the ballpark, delivery trucks unload cardboard boxes of peanuts,

pretzels, hot dogs, buns, soda, beer, ketchup,

and mustard.  A forklift swivels like a large dancer.

A worker on a break braids her hair, drinks some water, then tosses a ball with a friend.

In the belly of the ballpark, the laundry room churns, and a man feeds piles of jerseys to the machines.

full load

Suds, clothes, and one independent sock flop up and down and around in the washer. The dryer growls and spits out uniforms, nice and hot.

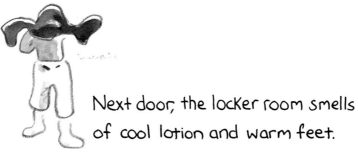

Next door, the locker room smells
of cool lotion and warm feet.

Players lounge on stools,
listen to the radio, and gossip.

One player dresses: socks, shorts, undershirt, buttoned shirt, pants, eye black, cleats.

He touches a ribbon taped on the door for good luck, and trots out to the field.

At the edge of the field, trainers stretch and twist players' bodies like gum.
The photographer stretches her tripod, loads film, and checks her light meter.
The sportscaster knots his tie and scribbles notes for his broadcast.

During batting practice, balls crack off bats and fly in arcs around the park. Players hide behind screens to protect themselves. One ball smacks into a screen, and a reporter jumps. Everyone takes turns: five swings, three, one.

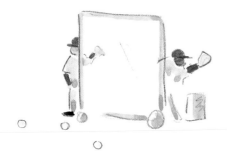

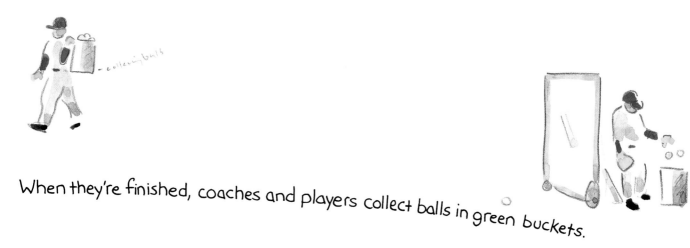

– collecting balls

When they're finished, coaches and players collect balls in green buckets.

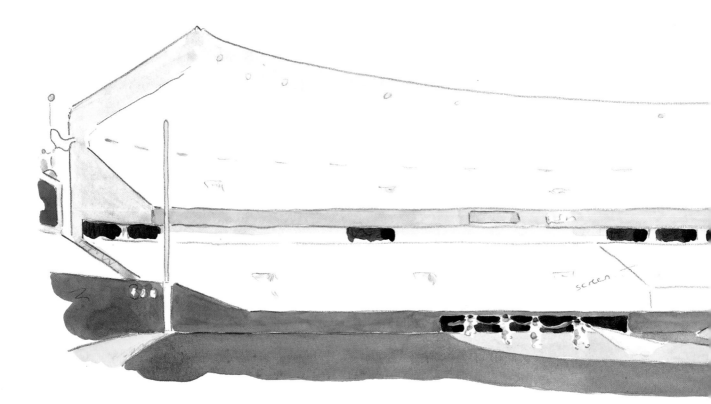

The teams saunter off the field, and the grounds crew races on.
A few rush around the bases with rakes, hoist bags of sand, fling dirt.

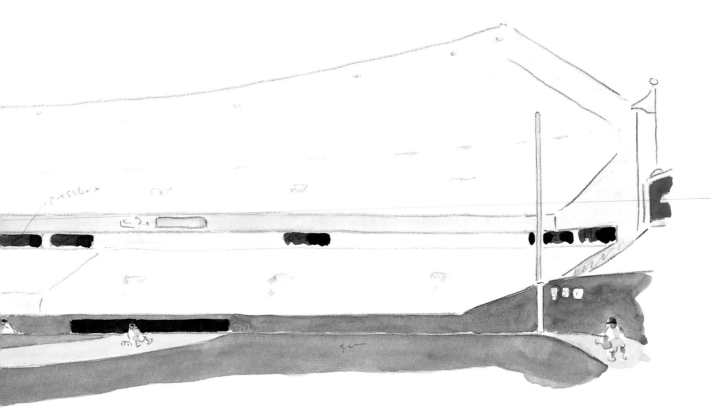

Two string lines and spray the base paths. One paints home plate.

The rest of the crew waters the infield with what looks like a huge lazy snake.

The gates open. Fans rush through turnstiles, ticket collectors snap tickets in two, and the crowd fills the park.

Flags rise in the outfield and flutter in the breeze.
A singer belts out the anthem slightly flat and misses
a few of the words, but no one seems to mind,

and everyone cheers when she's done.

The center fielder ties his shoelaces one last time.

The reporter sharpens her pencil. Play ball.

As the game starts, people throw food in the stands.

A vendor tosses peanuts. Another flips an ice-cream sandwich

behind her back. The floor gets so sticky with spilled soda

that people have to walk slowly.

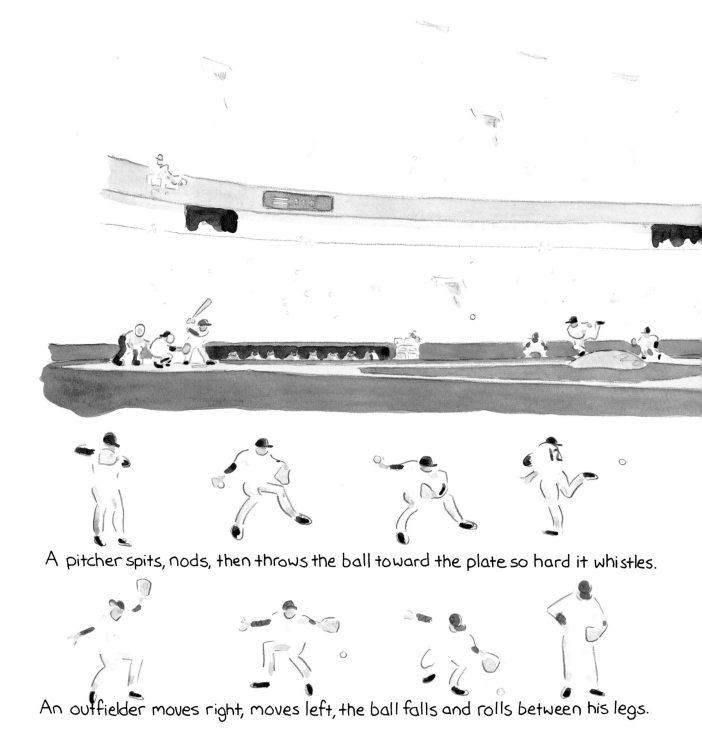

A pitcher spits, nods, then throws the ball toward the plate so hard it whistles.

An outfielder moves right, moves left, the ball falls and rolls between his legs.

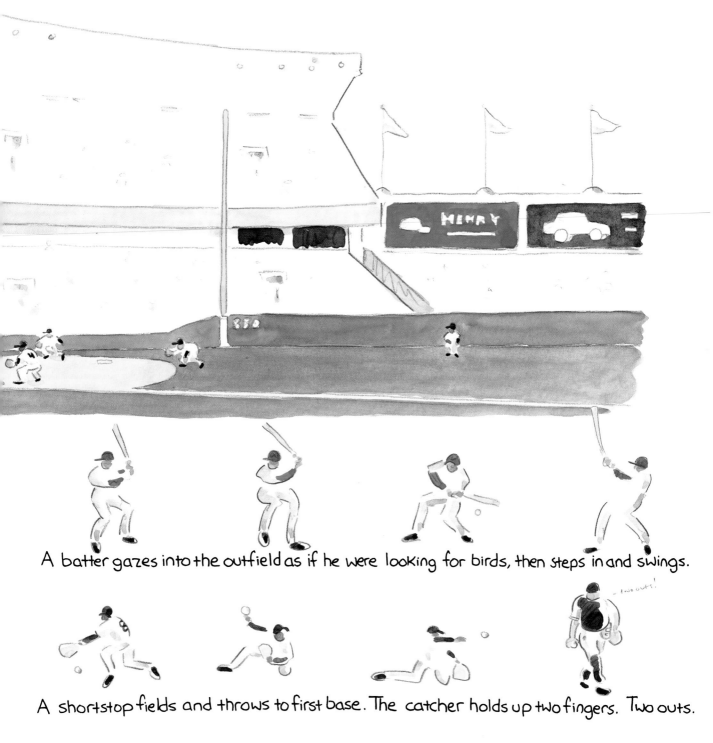

A batter gazes into the outfield as if he were looking for birds, then steps in and swings.

A shortstop fields and throws to first base. The catcher holds up two fingers. Two outs.

The umpire behind home plate
rests his hands on his hips as if
he just enjoyed a good meal.

The third-base coach signs to the batter. When the batter strikes out, the manager rushes

from the dugout to argue. The umpire and the manager get belly to belly. They get cheek

to cheek. They get personal, and kick dirt. The crowd boos. The manager is booted.

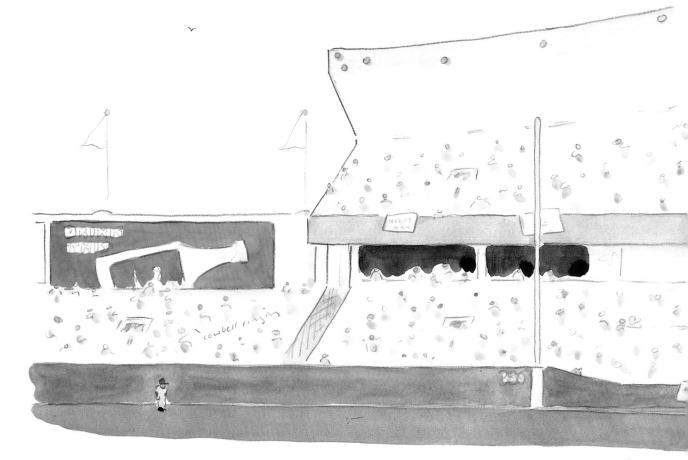

A foul ball loops into the stands past a man and his fishnet. The crowd laughs.

Down the third-base line, a ball girl dives and catches a foul ball. The crowd cheers.

A visiting player hits a home run so high it touches clouds. A fan throws the ball back.

A furry animal gets loose on the field. The crew tries to catch it and identify it.

The sky turns dark, then opens up and pours.

The grounds crew pulls a tarpaulin onto the field fast—

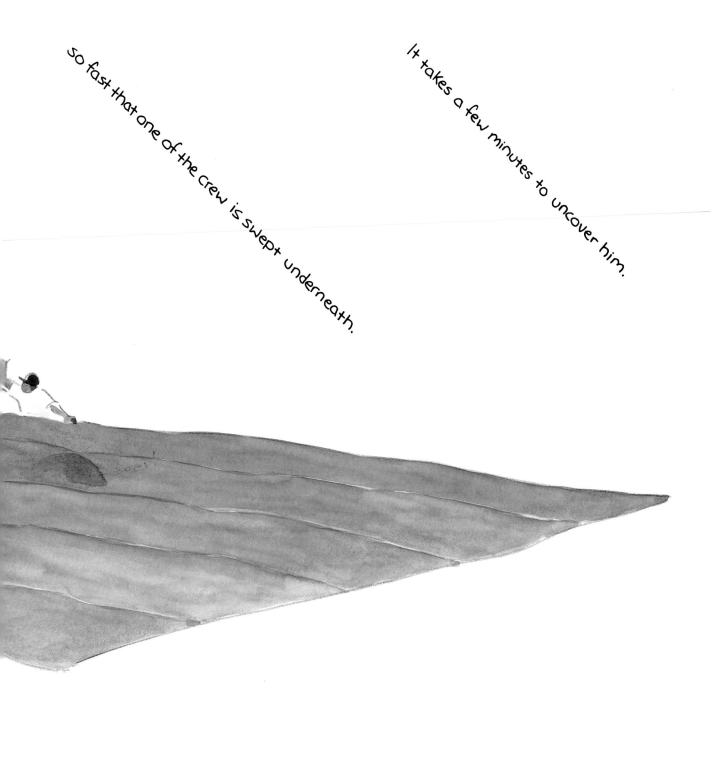

so fast that one of the crew is swept underneath.

It takes a few minutes to uncover him.

Players hang out in the dugouts and wait for the rain to stop. Some play cards. Others play golf using bats and balls with hats for holes.

Another fills a watering can for his basil and tomato plants.
One flicks and spits sunflower seeds at unsuspecting teammates.

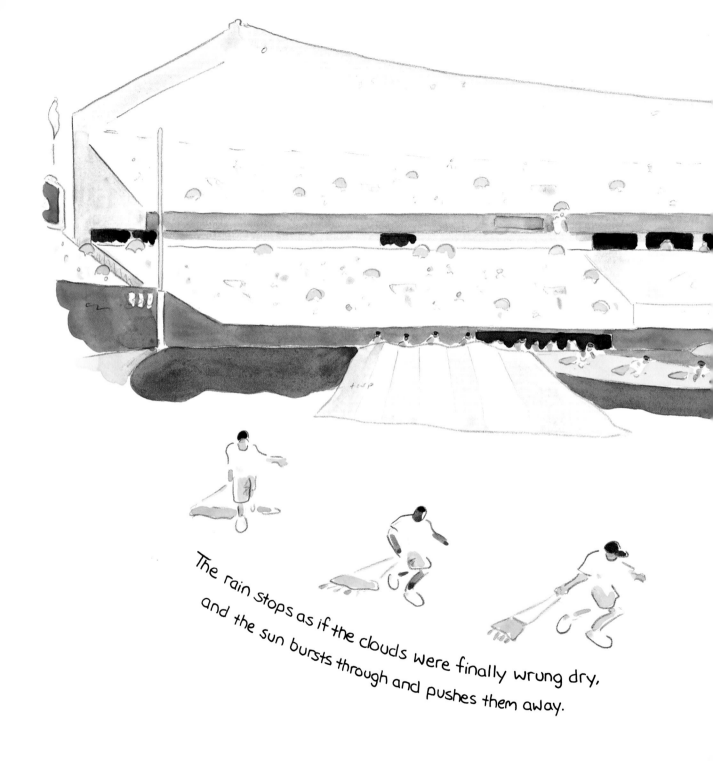

The rain stops as if the clouds were finally wrung dry,
and the sun bursts through and pushes them away.

Shadows lengthen, leaning out from the stands and over the field.
The grounds crew tidies up, smoothing the infield with mats.

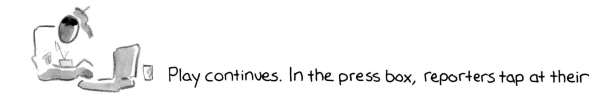

Play continues. In the press box, reporters tap at their computers. They drink coffee, drink more coffee,

flip and chew pencils, shout stats to each other,

and tell jokes on the phone to their editors.

During the seventh-inning stretch,

the organist plays "Take Me Out

hums along.

to the Ball Game," and one reporter

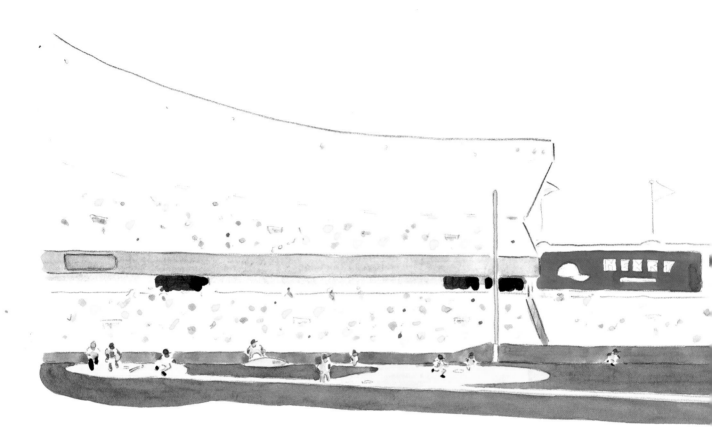

In the ninth inning, the home team is behind. The crowd gets to its feet as the batter walks to the plate. The batter swings and misses, and the crowd groans. He misses again, and the crowd shakes its head. Then he launches a ball that falls just past the fielder's reach, his teammate slides home, and the home team wins. The crowd goes wild.

The game is over. Fans have filed home, players have showered and left, and hot dogs and soda have been stored away for a later day.

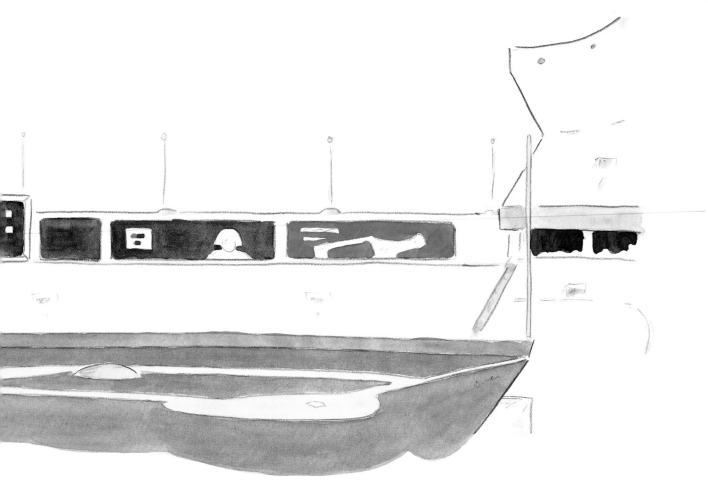

The ballpark is empty again. Outside, against the wall of the park,
a boy and a girl throw a ball until it's time for them to go home, too.

For Sophie and Henry, ballplayers

Library of Congress Cataloging-in-Publication Data
Cooper, Elisha.
Ballpark / by Elisha Cooper.
p.    cm.
Summary: Describes the activities that go on in all areas
of a baseball stadium both before and during a game.
ISBN 0-688-15755-6
[1. Baseball.    2. Baseball fields.]    I. Title.
PZ7.C784737Bal    1998    [E]—dc21
97-18756    CIP    AC